THE RED VELVET GOAT

A Mexican Folk-Play

by

JOSEPHINA NIGGLI

SAMUEL FRENCH LIMITED
LONDON

Samuel French Ltd
26 southampton street, strand, london

Samuel French Inc
25 west 45th street, new york
7623 sunset boulevard, hollywood

Samuel French (Canada) Ltd
27 grenville street, toronto

Samuel French (Australia) Pty Ltd
elizabethan theatre trust building
153 dowling street, sydney

Reprinted from " Mexican Folk Plays," by Josephina Niggli
Published by University of North Carolina Press

made and printed in great britain by
butler & tanner ltd, frome and london
made in england

FOREWORD

This is not a play, nor a revue skit, nor anything such as is generally seen on the English-speaking stage. It comes from the Spanish theatre, and is called a *saenete*. The dictionary translates it as a farce, but this is not a true definition.

The true *saenete* is simply a picture of what we call the " lower classes " lifted from reality to the stage. It is written in poetic dialogue, it is a comedy, and it has a romantic flavour. These are the general rules.

For this *saenete* of mine I have chosen the presentation of a home-made play such as one can see in any village from Quintana Roo to the Rio Grande. When a Mexican goes to a play he goes, not as a spectator, but with the firm intention of being as much a part of the drama as the actors on the stage. It is the prompter, however, who bears the full burden of the performance, and so, to him, health and wealth.

J. N.

The fee for each and every representation of this play by amateurs is One Guinea, payable in advance to—

Messrs. Samuel French, Ltd.,
26 Southampton Street,
Strand, London, W.C.2,

or their authorized agents, who, upon payment of the fee, will issue a licence for the performance to take place.

No performance may be given unless this licence has been obtained.

The following particulars are needed for the issue of a licence:

Title of the play or plays.
Name of the town.
Name of the theatre or hall.
Date of the performance or performances.
Name and address of applicant.
Name of the Society.
Amount remitted.

Character costumes and wigs used in the performance of plays contained in French's Acting Edition may be obtained from Messrs. CHARLES H. FOX, Ltd., 184 High Holborn, London, W.C.1.

THE RED VELVET GOAT

Originally produced by the Carolina Playmakers at Chapel Hill, North Carolina, on April 25th, 1936, with the following cast of characters:

ESTEBAN (who longs to own a goat) .	*William Chichester.*
MARIANA (his Wife)	*Hester Barlow.*
LORENZO (their Son)	*Robert du Four.*
LOLA (village Girls, friends of ESTER)	*Audrey Rowell.*
CARMEN (village Girls, friends of ESTER)	*Frances Johnston.*
ESTER (a village Girl with whom LORENZO is in love)	*Ruth Mengel.*
RAMÓN (a Pedlar of women's clothing)	*Holman Milhous.*
DON PEPE (the Mayor of the village)	*Gerald Hochman.*
DOÑA BERTA (a Neighbour and grand lady of the village)	*Janie Britt.*
OTHER VILLAGERS.	

SCENE.—ESTEBAN'S house on the Street of the Arches in the town of the Three Marys.

TIME.—Six o'clock of an afternoon in June. The present.

THE RED VELVET GOAT

SCENE.—ESTEBAN'S *house on the Street of the Arches in the town of the Three Marys.*

The late afternoon sun has thrown a golden haze over the patio of ESTEBAN'S *home. It is not a magnificent patio. There is no fountain with flowers banked around it, as in the home of* DON PEPE, *although there are pots of flowers on the stoop of the door which opens into a bedroom on the* R. *If it were noon, there would be chickens scratching about, and perhaps a baby pig or two, but it is evening, and the livestock have been closed up in the corral which is beyond the gate on the* L.

There are benches in front of us, and two rocking-chairs swaying back and forth in front of a platform that is made of planks resting on saw-horses placed against the outside wall of the house at the back. This platform, these chairs, these benches are not usually found in ESTEBAN'S *patio, but they are here this afternoon because he is going to present a play of his own composition. The platform is in a very convenient place, since there is a door leading into the living-room which serves very well for the actors to make their entrances and exits. That funny little box in front of the platform is for the prompter, and those grey blankets dangling from the rope attached to the posts at the two front corners of the platform serve as curtains.*

L., *now partly closed, is the great wooden door that opens directly on the streets from the patio, and if you care to peer through the iron barred window in the* R. *wall you will see* MARIANA'S *dress, which she intends to wear in her husband's play, laid out on the bed.*

The boy standing on the platform, clutching the stool in his two hands, is LORENZO, *very brown of eyes and skin and very black of hair. He wears the white pyjama suit of the tropics, with a red bandana knotted at the throat. Because he is twenty-two, old enough to have a sweetheart, he has on a pair of bright yellow shoes that frankly hurt.*

That woman standing R., *with her hands buckled on her hips, that flaming, flashing woman is* MARIANA, *his mother. Although she is forty there is no grey in the black satin cap of her hair; there are no wrinkles in the smooth golden cream of her skin; and as for her body . . . well, even the loose white blouse and the billowing red muslin skirt cannot hide the youthful fire in that pretty body.*

It seems almost impossible to think of ESTEBAN, *the man leaning against the edge of the platform* L. . . . . . *it seems almost impossible to think of this funny, fat little man as being* MARIANA'S *husband. Sometimes he wakes up in the night, especially after feast days, and wonders himself how he ever came to marry such a gorgeous creature. Poor* ESTEBAN *with his funny little blob of a nose perched in the middle of a round moon face, is no match for* MARIANA *and he knows it. His hands are always aimlessly clutching at each other. They are doing it now as he watches* LORENZO *with the stool.*

MARIANA (*impatiently to* LORENZO). No, fool! Where are your brains? Remove the chair and place it in the corner to the right. Esteban, speak! You are the master of the play.

ESTEBAN. To hear you rattle on, a man would think it was your scene. (*He points* L.) The stool goes there.

MARIANA (*points* R.). No, there! Would you have it hide the door?

ESTEBAN (*angrily*). I say it goes there! Lorenzo, place it where I say or I will break your head!

LORENZO (*who, through the argument has been standing still patiently holding the stool, now bangs it down in front of him on the platform*). Holy saints! Whom am I to obey? I'll put it here, and you can change it where you like. I am an actor, not a doll on strings. I must go read my part again.

(*He goes out through the platform door, slamming it behind him.* MARIANA *hides a laugh.*)

MARIANA. He says he is an actor. Haha! Then I am queen of tragedy. What hour does it grow to be?

ESTEBAN (*taking a large gold watch from his pocket*). My watch says eight, so then it must be six. (*He bends towards her, clasping his hands tightly together.*) Does all the world know of the benefit?

MARIANA. Musicians played before each door in town. I sent Lorenzo out with notices this morning. Do you think our guests will pay enough to buy a goat? (*She sinks down on the end of one of the benches.*)

ESTEBAN. We only need ten pesos for a goat. Don Pepe said he'd sell us one of his. With the money from its milk and cheese we'll have enough to buy another one, and soon we'll have a flock. Then we'll be the richest two in town.

MARIANA (*scornfully*). Just with one goat? What silken dreams you can build from air. To hear you speak no man in all the northern part of Mexico will be so rich as you when this play is done.

ESTEBAN (*with modest pride*). My talents are so varied, Mariana. Perhaps we should not buy a goat at all. Anyone can own a goat, but I, and I alone, can compose such drama.

MARIANA. A truth, a little truth indeed, my 'Steban. No other man could write such plays (*she flares at him*) . . . because he would not write them. I think it best to buy the goat.

ESTEBAN (*shocked*). Have you no soul, no breath of genius blowing through your feeble brain ? In time the world shall hear of this Esteban and mourn the fact that he possessed such a blockhead for a wife.

MARIANA (*peeved*). Who gave you hints of how to write it best but me, me, me ! Who furnished you with chairs, and clothes, and men ? Yes, men ? (*She goes to him, her eyes burning with anger.*) Lorenzo is my son as much as yours. Oh, when I wept and cried the night that he made his first entry in the world I did not think that he would grow to be an actor.

ESTEBAN. Do not fear. My son has failed to grasp my talent. He . . .

MARIANA. Is better, far, than you will ever be.

ESTEBAN (*grandly ignoring her*). Did you bring the vase from Doña Berta's ?

MARIANA. It is on the table in the house next to my red and blue one. You see, I do not forget, even if you do.

(*She goes into the bedroom* R.)

ESTEBAN (*following her to the door and calling after her*). Now what have I forgotten ?

MARIANA (*from inside*). Just a prompter, that is all.

(*She enters, goes to the platform and places the vases on the prompter's box, standing back to see the effect.*)

A little prompter to aid us with his book when we forget.

ESTEBAN (*with a gasp*). I meant to ask Don Pepe . . .

MARIANA (*sarcastically*). Did you indeed ? Don Pepe, the mayor of the Three Marys ! Perhaps you would prefer to have the President of the Republic, or the great civil judge to read our lines for us ! Where are your wits, fool ? Hanging from your nose like Spanish moss upon an ancient wind-blown tree ?

ESTEBAN (*wringing his hands*). It grows near the

hour of our performance ! Why did you not remind me of this small detail ?

MARIANA (*flinging her arms above her head*). Remind you ! Saints in Heaven ! Holy Mary aid me ! Oh, what ass is this dressed in man's clothing ? Must I remember everything ? Or was the play of your invention ?

ESTEBAN (*maliciously*). Who gave me hints of how to write it ? Who gave me chairs, and clothes, and men, but you, my little, darling wife ?

MARIANA (*furious*). But even I could not give you wit, my love. Each day I watch your ears grow longer and more pointed. Some day they will fall down and slap your cheeks, like that (*she gives him a resounding slap*) . . . and then you will remember Mariana.

ESTEBAN (*ruefully*). You are the whip I wear here at my belt, my sweet (*he rubs his face*) . . . a whip that does not need my hand to wield its power.

MARIANA. Enough of arguments. The crowd will soon be here. Go out and hunt a prompter.

ESTEBAN (*scandalized*). At this hour ? Have you no thought at all for my great art ? Am I not the hero of this play ? In a short time I must walk across that stage, and even now my poor heart is beating in my chest, and see my hands (*he wiggles them loosely*) . . . shaking at the wrist.

MARIANA (*firmly*). Am I not the tragic lady of this play ? I will not speak a line of your great drama until a man is safe within that box.

ESTEBAN (*imploring aid from Heaven*). Why did I marry such a woman, who loves an argument more than her soul's salvation ?

MARIANA (*also imploring Heaven*). Why did I marry such a lazy fool, who would rather sit in the sun and watch the goats feed on the mountain-side than make an honest living for his family ?

(LORENZO *opens the platform door and sticks his head through.*)

LORENZO. There are some people coming up the hill.

MARIANA (*giving a startled shriek and running towards the bedroom door* R.). The audience! And I not dressed!

ESTEBAN (*stopping her*). Mariana, Lorenzo can find the man we need. (*As* MARIANA *pauses, he turns to* LORENZO.) My son, we need a prompter. Go into the town and search for one.

MARIANA. Bring back a man who can read, and not some ignorant fool.

LORENZO (*coming out on the platform, a large square piece of red velvet in his hands*). I have already spoken to Don Pancho's son, Ramón. The one who peddles silks and threads to all the women in the towns near by. He can read, yes, and write, too.

MARIANA (*her eyes fixed on the velvet, and speaking in a strangled voice*). Lorenzo! Lorenzo, for what is that red velvet?

LORENZO (*innocently*). To cover the prompter's box, my mother, so that all the world shall know we give a play.

MARIANA (*stalking up to the platform*). Where did you get it? Where did you find that strip of goods?

(ESTEBAN *frantically signals to* LORENZO *to keep quiet.*)

LORENZO (*looking curiously at his father*). What is it, sir? Why do you not speak out? I cannot read such wavings of the hands.

(ESTEBAN *sinks down on one of the benches with a helpless gasp.*)

MARIANA (*swings on him*). So! It was you who gave it to him, eh? Well, search your brain for clever, useless answers. Where did you find the velvet?

ESTEBAN (*pleadingly*). Mariana, you have not worn that dress in many years. Not once have you worn it since our wedding day.

MARIANA (*slowly*). My dress. My beautiful red

dress. The dress I wore when I first met the man I loved. (*She glares at him.*) From which part did you cut it?

LORENZO (*helpfully*). From the back. (*He turns around and makes an effort to show her how high up the cut came.*) You could replace the goods with a piece of red silk. Besides, when you are talking to your friends, they would not peer behind to see the difference.

MARIANA (*bursting into tears*). Oh, love of God and all the little angels! When was a woman so afflicted with such fools for a family?

ESTEBAN (*awkwardly patting her shoulder*). I know, my sweet, my heart's queen, my little cooing dove, that you have kept it out of sentiment. But you have other gowns that you first wore at our early meetings.

MARIANA (*jerking away from him*). I said I wore it when I met the man I loved, not the ass I married! (*Blazing out at them.*) Get out of my sight, the two of you! Oh, saints in Heaven, you and your plays and goats, and my red velvet gown. (*Her voice drops to a quiet deadly tone.*) I will make you pay for this, my friend.

(*Girls' voices are heard in the street.*)

LORENZO (*excitedly*). We must draw the curtains. The audience arrives.

MARIANA. Will you leave before I break a piece of wood across your heads? (*She screams.*) Get out!

ESTEBAN (*jumping up on the platform*). We had best leave, my son. Your mother feels a little nervous.

(*As they start out* ESTEBAN *looks at* MARIANA, *who has walked to the gate* L. *and has her back turned to them. He runs to the prompter's box, drapes it with the velvet, then hastily pulls the curtains as the girls appear at the gate. He and* LORENZO *disappear through the platform door.*)

MARIANA (*opening the gate*). Enter, enter. Our house is yours.

(ESTER, LOLA *and* CARMEN *enter. Their skirts are of striped material, their blouses very white and clean. Their hair falls in two plaits over their shoulders and they possess the wild, shy beauty of young deer. All three have on shawls. When they speak their voices are high and shrill and sweet, and they have the habit of giggling behind their hands.*)

ESTER. Here is our money, Doña Mariana.

LOLA. Will Lorenzo play a part ?

(*All giggle at* LOLA'S *boldness.*)

MARIANA (*beaming on them*). He will indeed.

CARMEN. May we sit anywhere we like ?

MARIANA (*nodding*). Wherever you may choose to sit save in the rocking-chairs. They are for Doña Berta and Don Pepe.

(*The girls giggle as they find their places.* RAMÓN *comes to the gate.* RAMÓN *is very handsome and knows it. He wears a stiff straw hat, a bright pink shirt, a black tie, brown trousers, and shoes that are more orange than yellow, with button tops. His voice drips with personality.*)

RAMÓN. Is this the house of one Esteban Elizondo? Is this the house where there will be a play ?

(MARIANA *gazes thoughtfully at him. To her, any new man is subject to conquest. It is perfectly harmless. She has never been unfaithful to* ESTEBAN. *She just likes to know that she could be if she wanted to.*)

MARIANA. So you are old Don Pancho's youngest son, Ramón ?

RAMÓN (*making her a low bow*). Your servant, señorita.

MARIANA (*smiling faintly*). I am Lorenzo's mother.

RAMÓN (*stepping back*). Impossible ! Why, you do not look so old as he. (*He lifts her hand.*) Allow me to press a kiss upon your hand from my dirty mouth.

(ESTEBAN, *sticking his head through the curtain, sees this gallant gesture and glares at them.*)

LOLA (*tittering*). Good evening, Don Esteban.

ESTEBAN (*grumpily*). You may not speak to me. I am not here. I am behind the curtain. (*Trying to show his authority.*) Mariana! Take his money and let him in.

MARIANA (*shrugging her shoulders*). He is the prompter.

ESTEBAN (*snapping at her*). Then he should be safely in his box, and you changing your gown. I will not have you roll the eye at every man who comes along.

RAMÓN. Would you be jealous of me, Don Esteban, and I only a poor pedlar of woman's goods?

ESTEBAN. I trust no man when Mariana rolls the eye. Lorenzo will stand at the gate.

(LORENZO *sticks his head through the curtains below* ESTEBAN'S.)

CARMEN. Good evening, Lorenzo.

(*The three girls giggle.*)

LORENZO. Good evening, Carmen, Lola . . . (*He gives a deep sigh, for he is in love with* ESTER.) . . . Good evening, Ester.

ESTEBAN (*sharply*). You may not speak to them. Are they not the audience? Are you not on the stage? You must stand at the gate and take the money in your mother's place.

LORENZO. But I cannot stand at the gate and learn my part.

ESTEBAN (*yelling, since the poor man is irritated beyond endurance*). You should know your part! You will stand where I direct you.

(*He gives him a push, and* LORENZO, *who is holding the curtains, swings out, falling off the platform, taking curtains and* ESTEBAN *with him. The girls scream and stand up on their bench.* MARIANA *and* RAMÓN *laugh.*)

ESTEBAN (*from below the mass of curtains*). Help us up!

LORENZO (*wailing*). Ay, Father, you are sitting on my stomach.

MARIANA (*strolling over to the jerking heap of curtains*). Do I stay and take the money, my dear love?

ESTEBAN. You will change your gown.

RAMÓN. Here comes Don Pepe climbing up the hill. He will enjoy this drama. Not every hero can be wrapped in blankets.

(*A low murmur of voices from the road at* L. *can be heard growing louder and louder.*)

MARIANA. Speak quickly, my sweet turnip.

ESTEBAN (*frantically fighting with the curtains*). Help me up and you can own the goat.

MARIANA (*trying to hide her laughter*). Will you lend your hand, Ramón?

RAMÓN (*making her a deep bow*). For you, dear lady, I would cage the sun in a crystal lamp, and borrow a star's five points to bind your hair.

LORENZO (*moaning*). Father, will you get off my stomach?

ESTEBAN (*as* RAMÓN *helps him up*). I will, when peddling fools remember how to act instead of speaking airy verses to the moon's left ear. (*Moving threateningly toward* RAMÓN.) As for you, my fine friend . . .

MARIANA (*hastily*). No time for speeches now. Aid Lorenzo with the curtain.

LOLA. May we help?

MARIANA. You may indeed with Don Pepe at our gates. I will hold him off until the task is finished.

RAMÓN (*gallantly*). My arm, lady?

MARIANA (*taking it with a smile meant to infuriate* ESTEBAN). Thank you, Ramón.

(*They exit through the gate.* ESTEBAN *hangs over it gazing jealously after them.* LORENZO *is putting up the curtains.*)

ESTER (*watching* LORENZO). You are very strong.

LORENZO. In all the valley there is no man so strong as I.

LOLA (*helping* LORENZO *with the curtain*). So Ester said yesterday. (*She giggles.*)

ESTER (*snapping at her*). You have no right to repeat my words.

LORENZO (*forgetting the curtain and stepping down from the platform in front of* ESTER). You spoke of me . . . yesterday?

CARMEN (*helping* LOLA *with the curtains*). You are the constant subject of her speech.

ESTER. Who gave you leave to tell such tales of me?

(*She flounces over and sits on the bench.* LORENZO *follows her.*)

LORENZO (*softly*). Will you be at the plaza to-night?

ESTER (*turning her back on him*). I do not know.

(LORENZO *moves around to see her face, but she promptly turns her back again.*)

LORENZO. If you are there, will you walk around with me?

ESTER (*pleasantly shocked*). Alone?

LORENZO (*boldly*). Alone. Three times around.

ESTER (*gasping for breath*). But that would say to all the world that we were engaged!

LORENZO (*sitting beside her*). My father soon will have enough to buy a goat, and then two goats, and then a herd. He will give me money to buy a wedding gown for you, and slippers . . . small white slippers.

(*As the final tantalizing bit, since any beggar could have real flowers.*) And orange blossoms fashioned out of wax.

ESTER (*turning away her head*). Who can marry anyone without a house?

LORENZO. We will have a house with floors of soft blue tile. There will be a patio with white flowers growing in it. And, at night, when the moon is shining, there will be a light of pure green silver on your face. The locusts will hum their scratchy tunes, and the grey mocking-birds will wake and sing to us.

ESTER. What will they sing?

LORENZO. Of other lands they've seen beneath the moon. Of dusky jewels shining on white arms. Of fields of flowers sweet in bloom. Night-blooming jasmine, and the pale filagree of oleander. Of lilies, fragile as your hands, and blossoming thorn too sweet for any man to know its fragrance.

ESTER (*moves to another bench and stands looking down at it*). Is that all?

LORENZO (*following her*). Perhaps they will sing of mountains like purple ships against the soft pink evening sky . . . of cities that are pearls on the golden breasts of distant valleys . . .

ESTER (*whispering*). Is that all?

LORENZO (*softly*). Perhaps they will sing of blue tiled floors, and you and me. (*He catches up her hand.*) Will you walk around the plaza, three times, alone?

ESTER (*facing him, and once again the flirt*). With you?

LORENZO. With me.

ESTER. To-night?

LORENZO (*stepping closer to her*). To-night.

ESTER (*drawing back—she hears voices in the street*). There is Don Pepe.

LORENZO (*catching her wrist*). But will you come?

ESTER (*jerking away from him, then laughing up

into his face). Perhaps! (*She runs up to* LOLA *and* CARMEN *at the platform.*)

LORENZO (*catches his breath, then flings back his head and begins to sing triumphantly*).

Shadow of our lord, St. Peter,
The river lures me,
The river lures me.
And thus your love
Would my poor love allure . . .
My love allure.

ESTEBAN (*turning*). Stop your cackling. Behind the curtains with you, and you, señoritas, to your chairs.

(*The girls giggle as they return to their bench.*)

LORENZO (*as he passes* ESTER *he whispers*). To-night?

(ESTER *tosses her head at him.* LORENZO *and* ESTEBAN *disappear behind the curtains as* DON PEPE, *the mayor of the Three Marys, enters with* DOÑA BERTA *on his arm. She is a large impressive woman, while he is a tiny spry little man. A crowd of men and women follow them. The men wear various coloured bandanas knotted about their throats, and the white pyjama suits of the tropics, while the women are in colours as brilliant as the birds of the jungle country. They are all in a very gay humour, ready to enjoy the play.*)

DON PEPE (*impressively*). I have not seen a play upon the stage since I was last in the United States. (*He leads* DOÑA BERTA *to the rockers.*) Good evening, Carmen, Lola, Ester.

LOLA. Do they have plays upon a stage in the United States?

DON PEPE. They have the photographs of people who walk across a screen and talk like you or me.

CARMEN (*giggles*). Oh, Don Pepe, what a tease you are.

DON PEPE. And what is more, they can make

their water hot or cold with merely the turning of a handle.

MAN FROM CROWD. Now, Don Pepe, would you play with us?

DON PEPE (*with a luxurious sigh*). Ay, it is an education to travel.

DOÑA BERTA. I prefer my own bed every night.

ESTER. Is it true that girls can walk with men, even though they are not engaged?

DON PEPE. It is indeed.

DOÑA BERTA (*scandalized*). A most immoral custom. Put not such foreign thoughts in our girls' heads, Don Pepe.

DON PEPE (*rising and making her a low bow, then sitting down again*). Always your obedient servant, Doña Berta.

MARIANA (*to* RAMÓN). You had best into the prompter's box, while I change my gown.

RAMÓN. If you need aid . . .

MARIANA (*tossing her head*). Then I will not call for you, my saucy lad.

(*She goes into the bedroom* R.)

(*As* RAMÓN *steps into the box the audience claps loudly. He holds up a modest hand.*)

RAMÓN. I am but the prompter, my friends.

MAN FROM CROWD. Long life to the prompter.

(*The audience claps loudly again.* RAMÓN *makes another bow, and lowers himself into the prompter's box.*)

LOLA (*whispering*). Ester, did Lorenzo ask you anything?

ESTER. Why should I tell you what was said?

CARMEN. We would keep your words as secret as a priest at confessional.

DOÑA BERTA. What would you keep secret, miss?

CARMEN. Ester spoke with Lorenzo all alone.

DOÑA BERTA (*scandalized*). What?

DON PEPE (*startled*). Eh ?

ESTER (*defensively*). Lola, Carmen, and Don Esteban were here.

LOLA. But just we three. That is almost the same as being alone.

DOÑA BERTA. That is your wild advice taking root, Don Pepe.

DON PEPE. Girls and boys must speak together. How else would marriages arrange themselves ?

DOÑA BERTA. When I was young, girls listened to their parents.

MAN FROM CROWD. Is that why you have remained a spinster, Doña Berta ?

(*Loud laughter from the crowd.*)

DRUNK IN CROWD (*sings tune of* LA CUCARACHA).

All the maidens are of gold
And the married ones of silver.
All the widows are of copper
And the others merely tin.
La cucaracha, la cucaracha . . .

DOÑA BERTA (*standing—she is furious*). Is this the gathering place of the drunks ?

DON PEPE (*standing*). Take out the fool.

DRUNK. I paid my money . . .

DON PEPE (*in his most thundering voice*). What did you say ?

DRUNK. I said . . . I need another drink. (*He staggers to the gate, then staggers back and shakes his finger at* DOÑA BERTA, *as he sings tauntingly.*) And the others are of lead . . .

(DON PEPE *signals to a man in the crowd, who drags the* DRUNK *outside the gate and then returns to his own bench.*)

DOÑA BERTA (*reseating herself*). Such common men deserve to stay in jail, Don Pepe.

DON PEPE (*flinging out his hands*). He stays in jail so much, Doña Berta, that he keeps his clothes there and calls it his hotel. I gave him the key to his cell, yesterday. I became quite bored with locking it to keep him in, and then unlocking it to let him out.

(LORENZO *sticks his head through the curtains. There is loud applause from the audience.*)

LORENZO (*grinning and nodding his head, then to the prompter*). Ramón. (RAMÓN *sticks his head above the prompter's box.*) Can you perform on the harmonica ?

RAMÓN. Alas, my only talent is for the drums.

LORENZO (*woefully*). But who will play the applause music ?

MAN FROM CROWD. We will sing it for you.

LORENZO. Thank you, my friend. (*He steps in front of the curtain.*)

AUDIENCE (*sings lustily*).

Now the duck is in the pot
Bubbling for the fire is hot,
Lifts his head and calls for savour,
Adds an onion for the flavour.

(*They applaud loudly.*)

LORENZO (*bowing and shaking his hands over his head to the audience*). This is a tragedy of laughter, and a comedy of tears.

MAN IN CROWD. Long live the drama !

(*Shouting and applause from the crowd.*)

LORENZO. Its story I need not tell you, for you will see it for yourselves upon the stage. We ask you to laugh where laughter is needed, and for your tears where you should weep. If you go home contented, our labour has been repaid. (*He retires behind the curtain.*)

(*More shouts and applause from the audience.*)

(MARIANA *strolls in from the bedroom, dressed in a brilliant costume and with flowers in her hair.*)

MARIANA. I am the heroine. Will some kind gentleman aid me to the platform ?

DON PEPE (*hastening to her*). May I be of service ? (*Whispering as he lifts her to the platform.*) Was there enough to buy the goat ?

MARIANA (*laughing*). Quite enough, my friend. Thank you. (*She disappears behind the curtain.*)

LOLA (*nervously tittering*). Oh, I am so excited.

CARMEN. Someone is pulling back the curtain.

(ESTEBAN, *a large straw hat on his head, a gaily striped blanket over one shoulder, and carrying a gun, now pulls back the curtains. There is loud applause from the audience.*)

CROWD (*sings*).

Beans and corn and sweet potatoes,
Add a touch of red tomatoes.
Forget your sobs and your great sorrow,
We will all be drunk to-morrow.

(ESTEBAN *strikes an heroic attitude. There is a silence. Again he strikes an attitude. Again there is silence. He leans over and knocks on the prompter's box.*)

RAMÓN (*popping out his head*). Eh ?

ESTEBAN (*impatiently*). Well . . . begin.

RAMÓN (*blankly*). Were you ready ?

ESTEBAN (*taking a deep breath*). St. Peter give me patience ! (*Thunders.*) We are ready !

RAMÓN (*lightly*). I have no book.

ESTEBAN. And you call yourself a prompter !

RAMÓN. No, a pedlar. (*Seizing the opportunity, he stands and faces the audience.*) Ladies of the audience, I have silks and satins, wedding gowns and gowns for mourning, threads and pins to make you beautiful . . .

ESTEBAN (*screaming*). Enough ! (*More quietly.*) This is a noble drama, not a sale of women's clothes. (*Calling through the door.*) Lorenzo, the book.

LORENZO (*tossing the book through the curtains*). Here you are, Father.

(ESTEBAN *hands it to* RAMÓN, *who sinks down into the box. Again* ESTEBAN *strikes an attitude.*)

ESTEBAN. Begin!

(*The prompter speaks rapidly in a clear, monotonous voice with the actors, but he is usually just a word ahead of them.*)

ESTEBAN AND RAMÓN. I am a soldier home from war . . .

AUDIENCE. Bravo!

ESTEBAN AND RAMÓN. I am the bravest man in Mexico!

AUDIENCE. Long live the Republic! Long live Mexico!

ESTEBAN AND RAMÓN. I am returned after twenty years to see my wife and child.

MAN IN CROWD. The Revolution only lasted eight years.

ESTEBAN (*glaring at him*). Is this my war or yours?

(*Here* ESTEBAN *reads one speech and* RAMÓN *another.*)

RAMÓN. How I love my beautiful wife . . .

ESTEBAN. I am returned after thirty years . . . (*He bangs on the prompter's box.*) You are ahead of me, Ramón.

RAMÓN. Did I know you were going to repeat? (*Reading.*) To see my wife and son.

ESTEBAN (*exasperated*). I have already said that.

RAMÓN. Well, say it again.

LORENZO (*sticking his head through the door*). Father! (*He crooks a finger at him.*)

ESTEBAN (*walking to the door*). Well, what do you want?

LORENZO (*in a loud whisper*). You entered too soon. We are supposed to be ahead of you.

ESTEBAN (*who is rapidly losing his patience*). I

wrote this play, and if I wish to be ahead of you, I will be first.

LORENZO. Mother says that if she does not enter now she will not act at all.

ESTEBAN (*who recognizes defeat when he sees it—sighs*). Very well. (*He comes down to the edge of the platform and speaks to the audience.*) Pretend I have not been here. I will return in a little while. (*He goes through the door to much applause from the audience.*)

(MARIANA *and* LORENZO *enter.*)

MARIANA AND RAMÓN. I fear your father soon returns from the distant wars.

LORENZO AND RAMÓN. Father? You told me that he died long years before I was born.

MARIANA AND RAMÓN. There is a weight within my breast. I have always felt it there before I saw your father.

(*Loud stamping noise behind the platform door.*)

I hear him now, the ghostly beat of horse's hoofs. (*She falls to her knees.*) Oh, Holy Virgin, save me from his wrath.

LORENZO AND RAMÓN. I will see who comes. (*He runs out through the door.*)

MARIANA AND RAMÓN (*she beats her chest*). Ay, ay, ay.

(LORENZO *enters immediately, wearing a false moustache.*)

LORENZO AND RAMÓN. My wife!

MARIANA AND RAMÓN. My husband!

(*They fall into each other's arms. She draws back.*)

I may no longer call you husband.

LORENZO AND RAMÓN. What news is this? What sad words beat against my brain?

MARIANA AND RAMÓN. I fear Lorenzo's father does return to-day.

LORENZO AND RAMÓN. You told me he was dead.

MARIANA AND RAMÓN. And so I thought, but in the cards I read of a dark man, a dangerous man, and he is very dark, and very dangerous.

LORENZO AND RAMÓN. Your speech has stabbed me . . .

LORENZO (*in a loud whisper to* RAMÓN). Speak louder, Ramón.

(RAMÓN *is laughing so hard his words are muffled.*)

LORENZO AND RAMÓN. My heart is rent in twain.

LORENZO (*to* RAMÓN). How can I hear you if you laugh, you fool ?

(*Both begin to shout, but* RAMÓN *wins.*)

LORENZO AND RAMÓN. I die, I die . . . I am dead !

(LORENZO *stretches himself carefully out on the platform.*)

MARIANA AND RAMÓN. Help, help, he is dead.

(MARIANA *kneels beside him. She lifts up her arms, then looks at the audience.*)

MARIANA. Silence, please. This is the sad speech.

MARIANA AND RAMÓN. Oh, saints in Heaven, protect me from the wrath of man. Guard in your arms this poor sweet soul whose only sin (*she gives a long sob*) . . . was loving me too much.

ESTER (*wailing*). Oh, Carmen, Lorenzo is dead !

LORENZO (*sitting up*). I will return to life if you will walk around the plaza with me.

MARIANA (*pushing him down*). Lie down, you fool. You are dead. (*To* RAMÓN.) What happens next ?

RAMÓN. You carry him out.

MARIANA (*in a loud whisper*). Lorenzo, this is where you go out.

(LORENZO *stands.*)

Walk like a ghost. Remember, you are dead.

(LORENZO, *in as ghost-like a manner as possible, vanishes through the platform door.*)

Mariana and Ramón. I am a widow once again. Oh, Heaven. Oh, Saints. Oh, Love.

(*She follows* Lorenzo *out.* Esteban *enters with his face turned to the side, proving that he cannot see* Mariana.)

Esteban (*to the audience*). You remember that I am home, so we will continue from where I was (*he glares at the platform door*) . . . interrupted. I am ready to begin, Ramón.

Esteban and Ramón. I bear upon my chest the scars of war.

(*Loud applause from the audience.*)

Once I was wounded . . .

(*Loud applause.* Esteban *holds up his hand.*)

Esteban. You are not supposed to clap there.

Esteban and Ramón. Once I was wounded, but my enemy was cut to bits, and now I am home again to feast my eyes upon the beauty of my wife. (*He knocks on the door.*) Are all within here deaf ?

(Lorenzo *enters, without the moustache.*)

Lorenzo. Father ! (*He falls to his knees.*)

Esteban and Ramón (*drawing back with dramatic surprise*). And who are you ?

Lorenzo and Ramón. Your son.

Esteban and Ramón. My son ? Your age ?

Lorenzo and Ramón. Nineteen.

Ester. Lorenzo ! You told me you were twenty-two.

Don Pepe. This is a play, child, not a truth.

Esteban and Ramón (*with a glare for the interruption*). A son of mine nineteen, and I from home for thirty years ?

Man in Crowd. You said twenty the first time.

Esteban. Did I not write this play ? If I choose to change the date then I change the date, with no advice from you !

ESTEBAN AND RAMÓN. Where hides the woman you call mother, and whom I once called wife!

ESTEBAN (*to the audience*). You can applaud for that.

(*Loud applause.* ESTEBAN *modestly waving his hand.*)

Thank you, my friends.

ESTEBAN AND RAMÓN. Where is she?

(MARIANA *enters.*)

MARIANA AND RAMÓN. Ay, Federico!

ESTEBAN AND RAMÓN. Ysabela, my love . . .

MARIANA AND RAMÓN. My husband!

(*They embrace.*)

ESTEBAN AND RAMÓN (*he draws back from her*). One moment! Explain how it is that I have a son nineteen, and I from home (*he comes down and glares at the man in the crowd*) . . . forty years!

MARIANA AND RAMÓN. I thought that you were dead, completely dead.

ESTEBAN AND RAMÓN. Kneel down.

MARIANA AND RAMÓN (*she kneels*). I was young and beautiful, and weak to a man's whisper.

ESTEBAN AND RAMÓN. I must commune within my mind, secret and alone.

ESTEBAN (*goes down and faces the audience*). What shall I do? What would you do, my friends?

MAN IN CROWD. Shoot her!

ANOTHER MAN. Chop off her head!

DOÑA BERTA (*in a trembling voice*). Forgive her.

ESTEBAN (*rapping on the prompter's box*). What do I do now?

RAMÓN. You choke her.

ESTEBAN AND RAMÓN (*returning and beginning to choke* MARIANA). So shall all men deal with unfaithful wives.

(*Loud applause from the audience.* ESTEBAN *bows and goes down to the edge of platform, shaking his own hands above his head.*)

AUDIENCE (*singing.*)

Hungry now the neighbour's look,
Stand and wait and watch it cook.
But, alas, they must not eat it.
Bravo! Bravo!!!

ESTEBAN. Thank you, my friends.

(*He goes back and finishes choking* MARIANA. *She falls dead.*)

ESTEBAN AND RAMÓN. So am I revenged. (*He kicks her.*)

MARIANA (*sitting up angrily*). That kick was not in the play!

ESTEBAN. Shh . . . lie down. You are dead.

MARIANA. Not too dead to deal with you, you ancient eater of cow's meat.

(*She reaches out and grasps one of the vases on the prompter's box and throws it at him. He ducks, and it smashes on the floor. She screams.*)

Ay, it was my own vase! I thought it was Doña Berta's.

DOÑA BERTA (*standing*). So I am not only insulted, but my property is destroyed as well. I stay no longer here!

(*She sweeps out of the patio with hurt dignity. The audience rises.*)

ESTEBAN (*wringing his hands*). But the play is not finished. I have still a beautiful speech.

MARIANA (*jumping down from the platform*). Say it alone! I am finished with your drama.

(*She runs into the bedroom* R.)

RAMÓN (*climbing out of the prompter's box*). As for me, I prefer a good bottle of beer in the saloon. I have money, my friends. Who joins me?

(*With much cheering the audience, with the exception of* DON PEPE, LOLA, CARMEN *and* ESTER *press forward to shake* ESTEBAN'S *hand, and then follow* RAMÓN *through the gate.*)

ESTEBAN (*sitting down on the edge of the platform*). My beautiful play.

DON PEPE (*comfortingly*). It was an excellent drama, my friend. I think that we can arrange about the goat. (*To the girls.*) Shall I walk home with these three pretty flowers ?

LOLA (*giggling*). Ay, Don Pepe.

CARMEN. Will you tell us all about the United States ?

DON PEPE (*beaming*). With the greatest of pleasure.

LORENZO (*who has worked his way around to* ESTER). Ester.

ESTER (*earnestly*). When you died I knew the truth.

LORENZO. Will you be on the plaza to-night ?

ESTER (*stamping her foot*). No.

LORENZO (*crestfallen*). You . . . won't ?

ESTER. Not unless you should be there too.

(*She runs out through the gate.*)

LORENZO. Ester !

(*He runs out after her.*)

DON PEPE. My three flowers have shrunk to two . . . one for each arm. (*He extends his crooked arms and the girls take them.*)

LOLA (*as they exit through the gate*). Do they have such beautiful dramas in the United States ?

(ESTEBAN *sinks his chin in his hands and takes a long sniffling breath.* MARIANA *enters, dressed in a bridal gown. She parades up and down in front of him.*)

ESTEBAN (*sighing*). The play is finished, but at least we have enough to buy the goat. (*He notices her for the first time.*) What are you wearing ?

MARIANA. A bridal gown, which you could see if you were not so blind, my fool.

ESTEBAN. Have I seen that gown before ?

MARIANA. I think not. It has only just been purchased. (*She preens herself.*)

ESTEBAN (*springing up*). From Ramón ? (*He catches her wrist.*)

MARIANA (*pulling her hand away*). From the pedlar of silks and satins, threads and pins, to make all ladies beautiful.

ESTEBAN (*narrowing his eyes*). With what did you pay for that gown ?

MARIANA (*touching her dress lightly*). With the money that I took in at the door.

ESTEBAN (*squeaking*). The money for my goat ?

MARIANA. No, my love. (*She jerks the velvet from the prompter's box and holds it out towards him.*) The money to replace an ancient gown of bright red velvet.

ESTEBAN *grasps his head and moans as—*

The CURTAINS *close.*

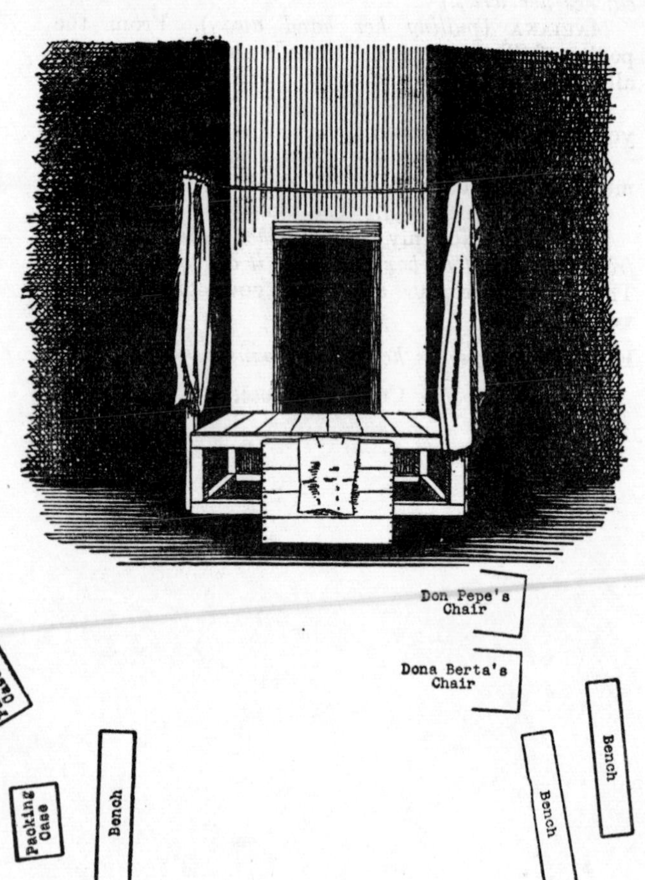
Don Pepe's Chair
Dona Berta's Chair
Packing Case
Packing Case
Bench
Bench
Bench